Think

As Your Heart Beats

Think As Your Heart Beats is an original compilation
of poems and sayings published by Aken V. Wariebi,
under the imprint of I-CAN Productions.
Please address any inquiries to I-CAN Productions,
P.O. Box 101, Fairport, New York 14450

Copyright © 2002 by Aken V. Wariebi

All rights reserved. This book, an imprint of
I-CAN Productions, Fairport, N.Y. 14450, may not be
republished, copied, reproduced or adapted in whole or
in part, in any form. The only exception to the above is a
review, in which brief passages may be quoted with permission.
Inquiries should be addressed to I-CAN Productions,
P.O. Box 101, Fairport, New York 14450.

Wariebi, Aken V.
Think As Your Heart Beats

ISBN: 0-9707503-0-7

Library of Congress number 2001-130004

First printing – February 2002

Photo on cover by:
Roger Leavy

Editor-in-chief:
Linda Heffron

Advisors:
John C. Viglucci, Summuh Nester Duncan, and Phyllis Walker

Think As Your Heart Beats

by
Aken V. Wariebi

I-CAN PRODUCTIONS

New Contact Information:
P.O. Box 20097
Rochester, NY 14602
585-234-1434
www.i-canproductions.com

Dedication

This book is dedicated to my grandparents;
Mr. James William Duncan and
Mrs. Sarah Sarta Burphy Duncan.
Their ambition and determination to instill discipline
through "hard-core love" expressed undying interest
in the building of character, values and focus in striving
for the best life has to offer while blooming where
one is planted. Their hardwork, love and faith in God
and their willingness to be a help to those in need
have inspired me in so many ways.
May their souls rest in peace and
those traits be passed on amongst
our generations ahead.

Acknowledgement

Intense gratitude to a source much higher with the power that provided me with the insight, and talent to produce such a project. To Mamma, Summuh Nester Duncan, to whom thank you is not enough for her unconditional love, sacrifice and support. To papa, Jones June Wariebi, thank you for everything. Despite the path fate led us through journeys with triumphs and beyond I love you. To all of my supporters known and unknown, thank you and as your hearts beat may you not only find your gifts and talents but peace, love and happiness. The struggle continues and before my heart is spoiled with hatred I willingly forgive.

Foreword

♡

Tell me

Dare to achieve, it is an instant threat, Dare to be quiet, it is a sign of unpredictability
Dare to be content, it becomes annoying
Dare to cry, there seems to be a need for extensive counseling
Dare to be hopeful, it is idealistic, Dare to explain, Oh Lord! it is a sign of being argumentative
Dare to just survive, there is a major problem with that
Live a reserved life, it is interogation time and inquiring why so many questions are asked, implies an attempt to cover up some horrible hidden, secret or a double lifestyle

Be spiritual, it is perceived as one's way to belong and become a religious freak
Dare to venture slowly, it is wasting of precious time, to love it is an effort to impress
Dare to be loved, then it is occupying someone else's place
Dare to encourage, the conclusion is a desparation for friendship
Dare to be ill, it is pretense or a call for attention, Dare to be honest, it is a sign of niaveté
Dare to be kind, it is considered a very stupid part of your personality
Dare to be jovial, there is silliness being spread, and a way of exposing oneself

To speak, a convenience of an oversight and persistence implies a talkative trait
Dare to be unpopular, automatically insignificant
Dare to be popular, the many names for this won't be said
Dare to dream, many attempts are created to develop impossibilities
Dare to acknowledge, it appears that validation shuns the obvious intrusion
Dare to have courage, it seems to be a terrible mistake
Dare to be aggressive, Ritalin then takes the place of a trip to a much scarier place

Dare to be intellectual, it is like committing a crime
Together with intelligence, there is certainly no good intentions found
Dare to be outspoken, it is that trouble is in the making
Dare to choose which battes to fight, then a weakling or a chicken becomes a nickname
Dare to fight all battles, a suspicion of violence alerts a cauteous police team
Dare to be frustrated, a mockery is made that seems to brighten the day

Dare to lack behind, stagnant, satisfaction is an expression of so many a face
Dare to be philosophical the enemy tries to seek ways to destroy for it is perceived that one is showing off
The more one struggles, the more one is pushed down, a determination to succeed is found disturbing
Too bad, I personally have to disappoint those in the world who pain when I succeed, I am simply a part of a far better regime

How dare you make all the assumptions? But really, I need not ask as I should dare you, wait to see how you'll end up, when you've experienced all that I've being through during my time. But maybe, by then, it'll be crystal clear, once again, how wrong the multitude can be oftentimes, especially when the listener is blind

Contents

SECTION ONE

Just Think ....Pages 1-12

SECTION TWO

Humanly Possible .... Pages 16-80

SECTION THREE

A Spiritual Side .... Pages 84-106

SECTION FOUR

Loving Words ....Pages 108-113

Africa

The land where civilization began
The land where much is experienced by strength
A land where courage prevails over pain
Where ambition solely reigns supreme
A place where education prevails evermore
Where determination in no way is closed

A place of history of chiefs and kings
A place of rich soil and people with the culture of the same
AH! This is the place I call home, THIS IS MY AFRICA!
A place with a vast history that can't be explained
Where much love is expressed more in action than in words

A place of more solitude than you may think
The place of my ancestor's birth
A part of me, a part of my entire heritage
Yes, this is my Africa!
A continent of natural beauty and wealth
With bright sun rays, a well lit-sky

With beaches of lovers and fields of dreams
With tribes and languages not yet disclosed
A proud people, where dignity lies
This is indeed the people of my blood
A continent where I come from
This is my first home, this you see, is my Africa

Our character spells out the genuine uniqueness of this land
If you are from another land, to visit, plan a trip to the motherland
We strive and winnings are very well blended
Though misconceptions create a lot of instant fear
This is the land of my right hand, A very hospitable land
I stand for my continent, where faith in God lies with every man

As I reside in other lands, forgetting my homeland is not my plan
Wars seem frequent to the common man
We overcome, eventually, coping as usual our very lifestyle
But with all said or done, for or to the continent
By hook or crook it will continue to stand firm

Race relations

We are all a part of the human race
With shades of dark and light reflections
We are all of the potter's clay
So friends let it remain that way

We are dirt, simply put, just dirt
Whether with wealth, fame or just a little steam
The fact remains like everything
We too in time unknown must pass away

We must consider our race, this is true
The reason must be not for shades of hate
We can think in our minds eye why the shades?
Acceptance of this fact is evident, we are all here

Relating to one another is getting along
Animosity and racism, bigotry and a lying tongue
Will be judged not down here, but up ahead
Race is a word but humans we always remain

Nature

Nature is lively year in and year out
We witness the seasons and watch it wear out
New beginnings are so very apparent there about
The wonders of mother nature so easily sought out

The ocean, the land, remains in their place
Sometimes due to crisis behaviour they create
They have their own limits and may disobey
The plants, the shrubs, and the wild life exists
They too in abundance a beauty is made

The people, the sky, and the air we breathe
Are all doing their temporary jobs and yes, so are we
The nickname for nature is of course mother
For she controls the universe definitely like no other

Consider all that is nature appreciate their style
For they can disappear before you realize
The earth and its people are also fragile
Let's not take this for granted but value all we have

The complete universe and all therein
Are basically fragile, it is so clear to see
Considering these issues let's be grateful and know
That we'll never miss the water till the well runs low

Life is no practice ground

A breath is given, a child is born
The parents proudly sing along
The hardships come and so does joy
The great predicaments move the song

The child is given privileges and grace
He grows from kid to adulthood quick
His daring ways and his mistakes
Are not yet seen or heard of late

Life is no practice ground, beware
Each step taken is worth a risk
For every journey or battle fought
The consequences ring this is no puzzle, bitter or sweet

Life is no practice ground for all
A child or adult must know the laws
Life is no practice ground at all
Remember now or else be lost

Choices

How often do we follow the tide
Of people, of places and fads in the crowd?
In doing the following we may not realize
The choices we're making as we try to oblige
How often do we go with the flow, hoping it is the right way to go?
We complain but we continue to cling, receiving the damage the curses it brings

Not seeing them as choices just hoping to belong
We may not thoroughly investigate all, but smoothly gleefully hang along
We never would stop to look back for the pros nor the cons, we just willingly abide
Most oftentimes it is so much clearer, if we stand in the distance and look just near us
When in actuality experiences of feelings are mixed, our choice should be concrete if we just say
The day doesn't matter, the times rarely does, the choices keep coming as everyone calls

We may watch and observe, learn and unlearn
May perhaps even pretend as we celebrate
Use the chances we are given in the twinkle of an eye
It is good when we first think of the consequences
All of which our choices may create
Being wise as we decide what to do in many ways

There is always an excuse or a reason maybe two
This most times we try to hope makes the justification float
We may say that we are humans, a convenience not common sense
Let's remember as we choose that the world only laughs never ever cries with us
So in choosing please be wise, that way we will avoid many cries
Just believing that our tomorrows are still so haunted by the choices made today

A loss

A loss is worrisome, it is painful to acclaim
Just let it slide be calm and sigh, like water does on a turtle's back
A loss not awesome, not a sore
Just annoyance, a related show

So let it be, don't acquire more
For we all have losses and not under the mistletoe
A loss, let it be, just move on slow
Let not the loss take all your toes

Foes are entitlements for the human soul
None is excluded we grab with hope
Continue walking upright completing each tasks
Put every effort, reflecting and giving it our best shot

Sweating from hardwork we let ourselves see
That losses may come but we have won the lead
A loss one may see as eternity
It surely doesn't have to be common in a society

Confusion, frustration, peaceful solution
Are all feelings included with anxiety
Whether loss of money, materials or life
A loss is still just a loss, and that is so right

Be kind, humble and not too behoofed
A loss can not be made easier losing those too
Be ye patient, and still walk upright
A loss for one may just be a sign of one's guiding light

Blindness

A sight requires eyeglasses for correctness
A pupil is needed for much strength of such
A sight may require going in the right direction
But as blind as a bat I feel the fever

How evil is wickedness
How horrible is cloudy vision
So blindly the innocent travels
So naive with good intentions

I've watched the salt turn into gall
I've seen the devil saw and pull the wool
All that was right and all that was sure
Because of blindness all continues to glow

Bewitched I stand alone punished and sore
Suffering I stand alone with really no cure
Naked I stand, have been seen by all
Plainly I'm vicious and this has been so

Old lurking wisdom, old acting class
Trying to fight a battle, blind to the core
How evil and vicious affording to try
Knowing deep inside loosing is all I've got
For gaining yes, gaining seems only to come from the outside

Don't burn bridges

With every bridge you come to cross
Every word you utter with love
With every inch of care you've lost
With every smooth transition cross
Do not pass the alter boss, by burning bridges of them all

With every sweat upon your brow
Every inch of wood adhere
With every living seed planted in soil
Every sting bitten by a bug
Don't burn the bridges that you cross

With every switch you make to stay
Every adventure seen but swift
With every mean transaction made
All the trials you will come to face
In every thing that happens in life's way

Never burn the bridges made, it usually can't be reversed another day
They may never come again your way, hold it close and have your say
They are opportunities for your sake, they can take you far away
They are healthy and to uplift, for they are the stepping stones you make
Treasure every bridge you make, for someday soon it'll all repay

For all to see...........

We achieve awards dripped with ribbons
We accumulate certificates in honor of our cravings
We receive prizes to prove our commitments
Our goals are then accomplished for all to see

We gather up wealth as a result of hard work
We do just the same by many other means
We strife with energy to do to all and please
There may be a gap or two along the way for a tease

The gaps get covered so conveniently
Our errors are then erased or so we think
This too is just for all to see
We try to do what we think is right

We do some wrong in the dark and according to our own delight
We preserve our goals with all our might
Our conscious remains hidden and not one can see
The actual truth sometimes is not perceived

For all to see the praises we've gained, may very well not be the fate we see
Play on with this game for everyone to see
But live with the truth and the false that lingers and remain
Know in all reality, as much that is seen, it is not only humans that see

Yesterday

Back yonder things weren't as clear
Pressures weren't as much
Back yonder safety not such a concern
Hatred not a question or was it in demand?

Yet back yonder mistakes were still made
Corrections taken and relayed
That was then, this is now
Those were the good "ole" days

Back yonder prices not so high
Honour was to oblige
Status to respect, weather to comply
Schools were for teachings

Examples humbly showing
But all of this was yesterday
A vital portion not worth forgetting
For that makes for impressions and foundations used today

Back yonder people could wonder
Be honest, imaginations could be inspired
Yesterday the qualities were in the hours
The paths though cloudy had less rough edges

Today it is much different, and it is apparent
Yet we cope and mark the differences in appearance
But things have changed and better or worse
This is today and for the markings we still remember yesterday

What divides us?

Is it our status, our class or our race?
Our dreams, accomplishments, or fame?
Our education, ignorance or who do we blame?
Wealth, power or quite simply our origin?

Is it our laws or cultures that set us apart?
Our beliefs and values that help us survive?
We cry for justice but separate
Then stand aside witnessing division and splits

We attempt or create ways of escape,
The consequences we see each and everyday
So why not face the music as it is?
Accept each other and assimilate?

Every so often we see a rainbow,
The lesson is the awareness of our similarities,
For as the rainbow, we're of different shades
This makes our world a more beautiful place

So what divides us? You and I?
This question is not so often asked.
Is there no answer, or to be bothered we are not glad?
Let's not wait too late to find the answer searching first the hearts of especially you and I
Maybe then we'll figure out willingly, I might add, the basis of how we can be united putting prejudices aside

America

The land of the brave and the strong, where promising futures are capitalized on
A land of plenty then of none, where law keeps peace and goes beyond
A land of the determined to survive, where all is right yet can be wrong
Yet for the lazy a bag of waste, a defeated route some may say
Is a land, equalizing many besides

Not dying young, an impromptu field of gold
A palace for the destitute
A place of refuge and to renew
America is what it is called a land of promise for them all
A land where peace won't cry for help

But understanding is so diverse
Where features are not a facial glaze
But lying still sometimes a trick
America, the land of precious diamonds sunset blaze
Where youthful intuitions blend, and come together becoming a twill

For the helpless to be helped and the homeless to rejoice
Assistance offered and received by those who want and decline by the deserving inhabitants
America, a power, dapper piece of land
That streches a hand in every land
Today relive the motive friends

A rich history with records kept, a long commitment for the Library of Congress
Success is here if one would prefer it, no matter how they want to define it
Extremity and moderations, inclinations and every other commotion
Compassionate, cautious, and comprehend, listen, look and learn the plan
Relax, take a thoughtful step knowing the value, the purpose of this land where chance may define accumulation

We learn from proverbs,
folklores and sayings.
Quotes too included
not brown-nosed
and sliced.

Quotes

To be lost, stupid and blind can be created unintentionally. Know that the end result can still be something good.

❤ ❤ ❤

Hatred is so common in the universe, specifically earth. Love seems to have become stagnant, if there is any unconditional love left it is very scarce. Maybe that is why the word love is now used so loosely.

❤ ❤ ❤

Realization can be a rude awakening when perceived as ideology.

❤ ❤ ❤

The presence of poverty in the midst of riches reminds us that all is vanity.

❤ ❤ ❤

The presence of evil amongst good is a reality of wickedness and a reminder that it will always exist as long as there is good.

❤ ❤ ❤

Surviving the journey of life despite the complexities of the path we choose is an effort with a will.

❤ ❤ ❤

Knowing is better than not knowing. We can truly justify the reason for each. The reason, however, may or may not be the real excuse for either one or both.

❤ ❤ ❤

Life is a stage, only we are not actors. We each have our space to occupy and have only one shot to do it. One shot folks is all we are ever going to get. We definitely have no practice grounds or a how-to-manual. We can only give it our best and nothing else.

❤ ❤ ❤

Don't ask me why I cry, find out how you can make me stop.

This section is dedicated to all victims
and those who have been victimized.

It is only when we are
the most comfortable that we
feel somewhat satisfied, it is the
time we feel we have the most
accomplishments and security,
and yet it is truly the time
we should be most
on our guard.

Starting Over

From this day forward I begin again
Not as a wounded child I bleed
But like a brave strong person I plead
I am willing to begin again and crave the chance
I am starting over and now proceed

Please pardon me for the damage done
Though it may be partial it is only me I have to blame
I await the final call, my heart is racing now once more
I am starting over, I believe
Starting over comes natural to me

I look out yonder and can not see
Looking behind is erased from the scene
With errors made and joys entailed
Here I am starting over not a story just being relived
From this day forward, I now begin

Only to one option I now cling
Doing that right now an ultimate aim
Peace in my heart love for all, doing better now knowing better
Marching onwards, with precious jewels
I begin again, not like the child I once was
But the entire much more mature person that I have now become

Coping

When the tides are high in the ocean
Danger lurks in every wave
When the sea is calm
Peace prevails

Life seems to be that way each day
When trials quickly come one's way
But what will your reaction be?
To stare, or snare or intercede?

Will you let it break your inner peace?
Or help you to in God retreat?
To swear, or dare or quiver with fear
Defeat yourself by doubting self

A thought to carry on each day
Is to look up above and pray
And think of all the ocean swells
The folks who died and those who lived

Remember too to try and cope
As best you can through trials and pain
For through it all have peace be still
For only through that does peace prevail

Hope is alive

A word that has substance poise and grace
Provides ambition, not proclamation or hate
A sign of relief from an evil twin
Surely an earthly piece of heaven sinking in
Gives passion to the lovely at heart
Surviving tricks to the not confused but adjusted mind
Alive and well in this heart of thine
Hope… surpasses high above the ocean swells
Higher than a mountain top, our lives say a prayer

A feeling of sheer bliss with no mistake
Creates a sense of calmness amongst the ignorant and irate
Like a sweet smelling fragrance of a lady of class
Is like sunflower and honey spread far and wide?
Hope lives each day if we seek it
The growth not stunted at all or a ghost
Within our very soul this seed is sowed
Hope we come to know is alive because we reap it, as we grow old

Hold on to this word even if the meaning you don't know nor understand
For the meaning from learning and by experiences turns gifts received in demand

A little too much

A little too much talking
Brings trouble is one's way
A little too much silence
Makes agreement a fair tale
A little too much revealing
Opens the devil's plan for you
A little too much of anything just isn't good for you

A little too much of playing
Says no seriousness in you
A little too much ambition
Sorts out all the best of you
A little too much of eating
We all see the end of food
In all of your doing remember a little too much of anything
isn't good for you

Blessings in mishap

Thank God for the sunshine and the glory
Don't forget, and be prepared the rain comes too someday
God is there too, He never leaves anyone alone
He gives us no more than we can handle it is comforting to know
He'll carry us through, the trials, the pains, which we're entitled to

He tests our faith, He loves us still, we may doubt this
Let's not, God is there, He knows what He is doing
He made us, He has our future, our past and present He knew
Trust Him still, doubt Him no more, love Him still
Brighter the days ahead, you'll see, and come to know

Thank Him for the mishaps, all the errors in the process
Be grateful, others are worse, by far, look around you
Thank God for the mishaps, He'll carry you through
Thank God, despite it all, for every calm a storm cometh
In every win, a battle is fought, and in knowing God
In knowing our savior, let's trust His love for us

Retaining dignity

There may be respect for you
Admirations not a stand-byers crew
There may be some respect for you
Respect also dignity if you choose

Wait not too many opportunities
For the first chance can no longer wait
Hop up and stand and fight for your right
Even perhaps what you're entitled to

Retain your dignity dear one
Not only respect is earned lately
Personal pride, respect and dignity
They all define integrity

Conquering fear

With feelings of hesitation we can not dare to tread
We are often told we can not do and this we hold very dear
For though our hearts and souls can let us know
To follow our own paths we sometimes dread to go

But what we fail to realize then is fear is quite a costly fair
So how to speak up, stand up and dream?
If we believe not nor trust our seam
How then do we live in pathways clean?

While feeling the satisfaction of our dreams
If we ignore our hearts desire and worship fear
Not knowing that is what we should ultimately dare
Becoming stagnant becomes a part, remaining backward our very lifestyle

We conquer only if we cling, we hold on losing not a thing
Supporting self, and pushing forward plainly explains
Determination guides us through the obstacles to win
Conquering fear is the first step to achieve

For each and every goal we hope and aim, so knowing ourselves we want to succeed
Don't listen or allow failure to come in, it creeps up on the heart out loud
Remember only if we let it, it won't subside, so think, watch and wish upon a star
For in trusting our instinct we'll reach our theme, finding our prize, winning the same

A blessing

Don't look at yourself as a poor soul
For your soul is not suppose to be so
You are a blessing to someone, you know
That is why God created you for sure

Don't see yourself as an invalid
A pitiful part of creation's weight
Don't see yourself as a mean old witch
Detaining your talents and grace given

Don't see yourself as a piece of clay
Gallivanting in the parade of grits
See yourself as a blessing to others
See yourself as a blessing maybe to one

See yourself for who you are
Who you were and who you could become
See yourself as a blessing
My child, you are a blessing to someone if nothing else

A time for healing

We all know that there is a time for everything
A time too for a lot of healing
A time to console oneself, letting faith do all of it's work
A time for forgetting the hurt that occurs

A time for healing has its place in our hearts
Like the minute on the clock we get to every hour
The wounds are closed , the scars get old
The present is ours with the future to hold

A time to let go of the anger, the pain
A time to keep moving then the closure is sealed
No time for regrets with no burdens more or less
The time slowly moves and we have to let go

Endurance

Presidents, queens, people of class
Paupers, beggars, people from Mars
Lovers, friends, enemies, jailers,
Liars, givers, all sorts of people pleasers

All of those who remain under the table
Squirrels, mouse in the trap, and squanderers too,
All endure roles of their various lives
Feelings of endurance a process to meet

Calmly climbing not the fig tree
Peace is accompanied by respect or a silent rage
Faith makes enduring quite obsolete
False is the kindness, understanding sin

With all of these steps to recovery
Enduring is really unknown to some men
Pass not the Bible have faith it will work
Read all the lessons, learn from the words

Know that if all is at rest, true wisdom only
Comes from above and God knows what is best
Enduring is so much more then winning the race
Enduring is passing most especially if one's heart sincerely
says so

Permanent scars

For days gone by wounds seal and die
The scars remain to erase not the past
How will the scars hurt or heal you ask?
When within your heart the devil refuses to leave

Where can this scar go but permanently?
For they are tiresome to carry and your shoulders are cold
Trying a strategy of a new episode
The scars spread and your entire body is in view of the sore

The stretching and extension of all covered wounds
Awaken your senseless odor that pours
Permanent it always was and forever will be
The scars that you owned up to not easily

The baggage is just as painful as the scars you behold
The surface looks fine but it is really a comical line
Permanent the scars, the wounds healed a while ago
These scars were permanent since birth, you just didn't know

A claim of innocence

Handcuffed and put behind the bars called prison
With no chance to express or clear my name
The legal man a distance yet not far
My attitude obviously has a question mark
I cry, but the tears have dried up inside me
My heart bleeds, while I naively think others can pardon me
Even if I did do a wrong, I am still human aren't I?

The funds are lacking to represent me
Pro bono attorneys are skeptical about meeting with me
The witnesses hide and avoid any court scene
All others believe I am deserving of the suffering I receive
A prisoner, I am now you see, but I am as innocent as innocent can be
Who hears the cries and screams of people like me?
I do have some rights, even if I committed...............

I have claimed many things in my lifetime
A few clothes and often I try not to allow my burdens to overthrow
I have claimed jewelry, crowns, titles, and fame
Praises, miracles, in all honesty I must admit, I've played some mean games
I will repeat so long as I live, some crimes are merely a terrible mistake
That doesn't mean I should get a slap on the wrist
But pardon me now, I do feel some remorse, most of all, I hope in my life to rehabilitate
I can only wish that I could undo the damage, and could erase

I wish I could bring back the time and place
I wish I could bring back the circumstances
I wish I could bring back the decisions made
For now I know quite honestly, and most certainly
I would definitely trade places only this time I am not the culprit

Tears to victory

For every tear you shed today
Know it will be replaced by joys unforeseen someday
For every heartache and despair
I beg you please don't run away

For every search of self-identity
All the questions of originality
Climb each step in dignity
Trust it will all end in victory

For every battle fought and peace made or unmade
Somewhere in the uproar there is victory
The stumbles, falls and with all the miseries
Is just victory being born in a queer way?

Stride, walk your merry way
Giving up, never use it as a trade
Tears are lumps of sugar, melting down your face
Jump for joy, allowing your tears to flow
Knowing that in time to come they'll become "sweet victory"

With sticks and stones

Sticks and stones are thrown at me
Because of the terrible errors of my ways
To be judged or shunned is not a fairy tale
I can suffer, I have suffered and I'll still make it

I need no ridicule; I have accepted responsibility for what I have done
I'd rather not have old garbage in all sizes tossed at me

I can spend a lot of time whether I am in or out
Just feeling sorry for myself and being hated by the world
Though others think they have determined my future
To change, on my part, could be good and fruitful
For starters, as I pray, assistance cometh and not the death penalty

I have paid my dues and have yet to loose
Because giving-up is not hope but a doomed conclusion for the crew

With sticks and stones that come my way
Instead of holding anger and a lot of rage
I want to do something good
Refraining from hanging around like a fool
I will build a house, make it a home,

Have it a decent castle in which to live
This is what I would do, what about you?

Keep holding on

The rope seems very tight but I am holding on
Reality is what I see at the corner of my eye
As incredible as it may seem, I too can hold on just the same
For holding on to all I have the good I keep, the bad won't last
Idealogy no such possibility for surviving is not curiosity
To keep holding on an actuality
Sincererity, honesty and a lot of possibilities

Keep holding on when all else fails
Hold on very well even if you slip
Please don't cry too long, if in fact you do
The tears are healthy still too much makes you look like a fool
Why bother remembering the struggles won
To hold on keep on thinking of the strengths not stolen close
Keep dreaming, waiting wanting good, but holding on not losing hope

A little adjustment

Just a little adjustment won't hurt you now
Just a little adjustment won't waste your time
Only a little adjustment is what you need
With a little adjustment you'll be just fine

Just a little adjustment and the world sees you
In a whole new light but you still shine bright
Just a little adjustment for improvement's sake
With a little adjustment you have quite a kick

Only a little adjustment is needed in you
It is needed in each and every one of us too
So as you get adjusted and settling grows
We should follow too making an even flow

Frustration

When it comes we feel it first, it gradually consumes our attitude
If we allow the feelings to control, it soon leads us into great arrears/outward blows
Yet and still, it is always there in all and everything we do
Letting it steal our peace of mind, changes us from plain to thorns entwined
Staying calm, coping and letting go, seems to be miles and miles behind

Frustration, cultivates outrage, anger and hurt
Which cultivates revenge, violence and regret
The circumstances in all this mess, will harm you and no one else
Betrayal, sure may be the cause of this, lies and hate and all in fact

How you handle this feeling of loss
How you deal, interact, and meditate, retain your class
Compromise, comprehend, exhibit your intelligence
Will break or make, will generate, will reiterate instead of retaliate
More than coping, you'll be showing every ounce of strength
Without knowing the ability, the possibility of power that you have to overcome

Just settle

Why not settle for pigtails, and bread?
Not lobster or scallops or some fancy fare?
Why not just settle for peanuts and tea?
Why do you want cappuccino and cream?
Why not just settle with what you already have?
Then make a bed and lie as well

Why not settle for higher dreams?
Maybe you could achieve with efforts unnamed
Regret not if dreams are not ever revealed
Only ask yourself, why not settle right here?
Only if settling here is what you would prefer
Ambition for you is as your mind is set

But rising above the odds is not feathered upstairs
It is only the drive you may have that may get you there
With others help, you bloom and you might as well
Just settle, who are you to dream?, they ask of you
But you know to do what you settle to win

Deceived by pretense

It usually shows in their actions
And most likely in their words
The combination of the two can really convince a man
They try their best to seek your pity or impress you in whatever way they can
You have to be on the look out for their constant scheme never ends

Don't you ever fall for the story they have?
It is tentative all of the time
And if you believe them the first time around
They'll feel it is a weakness especially if you are kind
Consider their stories and keep your guard up
By never ever giving them the benefit of a doubt

Make every effort their quest to deter for they have on their minds a calculated purpose, With your permission, they may think you are unaware
They'll then deceive you by pretending, always impressing to make you unwind, though your niceness they will admire
They'll then pounce upon your good nature with intentions not too very kind
Their nicest are often created to accomplish in their own interest

So be wise and open your eyes, for smartness can be constantly acquired
Know and remember in all your dealings there are always
The cons around us, who sometimes seem the nicest people, but can constantly and instantly fool us and deceive us by pretending

Thorns on the petals

Gasping for air and racing to the garden
The flowers were a beautiful sight to see
Never would I have guessed or questioned
That the beauty was the thorn I had so often passed by

Slowly I watched the birds sing in the garden
Gradually changing their song into a cry
Like fragments of life the puzzle began lifting
Yet I was so ignorant all the while

I felt something stick me and I didn't know what
I was blinded by the beauty till it hurt my eyes
I danced by the music singing in my head
Not wanting to accept the pain as I twirled

Thorns in the petals, this couldn't be
So thinking for a moment ignoring wasn't so grim
I couldn't yearn for a better garden
This was all I knew, was exposed to not much more
If one had told me things could be better I would have found it so untrue

Now I realize what I didn't know then
There never should have been thorns on the petals I touch
I was only limited to the exposure I had
I have learned better now and can do far better than I so often realized

Death

Oppression of oneself kills oneself
Depression derives from this
Hope leads where nothing can remain
God's patience remains our guardian if we cling

The choices we make He has to approve
To think, to eat we must include
Vitality, longevity, sincerity creates
Treasures not left behind but, proof of what we find

The light at the tunnel's end is bitterly pleasant
I know like all, not how the future stands
Hesitating, common sense, can reach for us the peaceful end
Have control but know of God's rules and obey

The support He provides and honour that class
Slowly don't let your legacy evaporate
Please don't be like those who ignore
For when the call comes you will have to go

Try this for size

If you think you have problems
Look that man in the eye
The only problem is he can't see you
He is and has always been just blind

You have a slice of bread without jelly or jam
Be thankful too of that and more besides
That woman at the river's bank last night had been starving couldn't you tell?
Complain not of the shoes you wear nor the size it often comes in

Scrutinize yourself and view in gratitude, if nothing else counts see you as blessed
A candid, cautious, careful look with much thanks given
Think if you had less body parts, a scar that could be seen or someone bit your ear
Would you be less the complainer or still grateful or in between?

For size, my dear, don't be alarmed by a hat that can not fit you
Belonging in a midst or crowd is not the thing to fix you
You have a custom made size, and it is about time you knew it
Control you, for that is your limit, let other sizes least concern you

Be proud of who you are

No matter what others may say or do
Be proud of who you are
Trust in yourself, do not delay
In your journey of self-discovery
Conclude opinions wisk away
But be proud of who you are anyway

Be proud of who you are each day
No man will be prouder than you but you
With every bump, mountain or hill
Every fall, snake bite or trip
For very sad momentum placed
With less confidence at stake

Know thyself if you will, even when your hope is frail
Don't sit back ashamed of you
Know you have some value too
Watch yes, talk yes, do a little of those two
In all your doing as you should
Just know who you are and mostly genuinely be proud of it
too

Give me a chance

The Good Lord did it and so should you
Give me a chance, for I know what to do
Yelling won't help me, nor scolding behind me
Let me be dandy, not wild and crazy
If for one second you find me a menace

I shall know then you are forbidden
Scream at no one not me in a lifetime
Then I'll just know that your time isn't worthwhile
So, give me a break, I am in no hurry
Give me a chance the Good Lord did it and he makes no mistakes

Shun all my pleasures, call them your ashes
Make them your vapor and give me no time
Write to the leader as you misuse my intentions
Learn me I beg thee, and give me a chance
I am not cunning, neither am I pretending

You will never know of my personality
If only you would spare me and give me a chance
Yes, I am capable, like any man, responsible
Without a chance, you can not know this not any other talent
I don't know you as well as I would like to

Give yourself a chance to give me a chance, you have to tell yourself this often
Then I will slowly and wisely listen to your demand, only if I choose to, I will try
Not your instructions but live up to who I am, rest assured this is like I would expect
I only prove to me and you here too, but not giving me a chance, rushes blood to my head
Believing that I can, doing what I can, just after the moment you have given me a chance

Let no man take thy crown

There is a design for each of us
A custom made up crown
It's specialty defines our being
With all that comes from thine

We must embark upon a journey up front
If this crown we have is willfully worn
We can not wear none other's gloom
For this is receipt of how we are well known

This crown is for relief in things
Its wearing signifies completion
A wholesome healthy sign of neat
A mere necessity on our feet

Let no man take thy crown
For that is all you have of renown
Don't borrow or deny existence carelessly
Of this crown worn by your persistence unknowingly

If there is much to then repeat
The crown is still the crown for thee
To lend it is to lose one's soul
But know to wear it makes the trumpet blows

Underestimation: an unrequested label

So unfortunate, that child will not succeed says the self proclaimed predictor
It is a pity, accept the fact that you're a looser, a failure to the human race
I give you no sympathy, no compassion, no chance to elevate
You are dumb, ugly, ignorant and above all a coward
You are a disgrace to your parents, an aloof being, put here for shame
I stand with tears in my eyes hearing these words but I know, I'll make it
You're not fit to take part in this conversation, a recluse, a cheat, born with stupidity

Unfairly put down, I stand with tears in my eyes, yet I know, I'll make it
I soon begin to believe these things of me, but deep down I know it is false
I stand with determination in my cries for help with borrowed clothes on my back
With courage, I will keep standing, with faith, keep walking and with strength, be brave
With God as my armor, with peace that surpasses all understanding
I stand with tears in my eyes and let the insults roll down my back
I will indeed be a success no matter what the circumstance, I'll climb that ladder too
Success is not for one man you see, many own it and mostly the underestimated hold it

Today I have become someone, the verbal predictions and abuse, a thing of the past
The psychological scars slowly fading away, other abuses too are leaving me
I have stood in awe of myself, my supporters too are just as beamed
I have fought to stay alive with God as my witness and father, I have won
The self predictors will not give up, I know this for a fact,

they never do
Negativity for those who see my mistakes as gifts stand back, watching, wishing for more
But God made me, He knew all along what I am, was and would become, so He kept me standing, believing never underestimating me

Courage

Through the eye of the storm
There is courage
In the field of dreams
Courage
In suspense or fear
Truth or dare, living in tears
There is courage

Yet the darkness comes
Still courage
With the strength that is found
More courage
In the dawn of the day
In patience I wait

There is courage in one day
We don't know yet should we say
Peace helps with the courage
Here as we stay and wait

Courage comes in not forcibly
Sneaks upon us, we could give up still
Courage a ransom, a price to pay
Courage is whatever we make of it

Remember me

I carried you in the womb
I didn't bury you though confused
I patiently, steadily, anxiously waited
Embraced you when I could

I laughed with you when you laughed
Cheered with you when you were glad
I spoke for you, envisioned you
Remembered you when you weren't near by

Remember me, your friend till the end
Remember me though lost and spent
Remember me, even though you don't have to
Just know that I can not be with you each and every now and then

But still I believe and I always will
Remember that I truly cared and always wanted what was best for you
I may be gone a day a year, forever perhaps but you will always be near

One day I will be gone, maybe never,
An everlasting goodbye will never be there
Just know you are loved and I am the one who will always care
Believe me when I say I loved you then and always will

A special thank you

To begin to thank you, I start anew
For all the sweet little things you do
For listening, loving and crying with me
Especially too for understanding me

A very special thank you, to you
A million times and more besides
For patience, mercy, all support
For just allowing me to be me

A great big thank you, once again
For acceptance of all of my ways
My imperfections, my charms and hisses
Your coping with my kind of personality

I thank you too for all you are
The thoughts of gratitude will not subside
For all you are and were just meant to be
Especially for the bond we hold that soothes

Perhaps it could have been.......

I thought life had only roses and then the thorns hit me
I panicked and asked God to save me and cried out to his name
I froze when tested and bad the days seemed
Looking ahead the bleakness felt and I said to myself
Perhaps it could have been......

I always had blessings, smooth sailing, reigning with kings
I never wiped my brow for anything, in my lap it fell right in
A blessed child, a hoodlum not, a pedestal is where I sat
The love for life was so intact, I never fell and knew much mishap
Still I often thought with future unknown, perhaps it could have been........

Little did I see selfishness, little did I see anything else
I gave advice to everyone, my own words hunted me not
I didn't know or realize how so selfish were my acts
When peace and joy temporarily escaped, I stood in awe none could relate
Any little thing quickly could irritate, Denial then was a popular mix
So instead of having faith, I allowed and let anger take the place

In its place was emptiness, lack of understanding and patience left
I saw like dust the future rest, many stared and wonder as I
None could explain, neither could I, but God was there all along
So now all I can say to soothe myself and still admit,
It was to be and God did permit, I should not question or have regret
I should not wonder or feel like I have neglect, nor even say to myself first
Perhaps it could have been any other way, for this is how God wanted it

Adapted to change

Adapting is difficult in so many different ways
First healing is geared towards adjusting like cake
The thought of transition the plunge and the dive
Pollution develops or sweet fragrances arise

Some changes are pluses some minus too
The middle not boldness but moderation sifts through
Diverting and pleading with self to divulge
Confronting illusions freely giving self some thought

Anxiety develops, panic and some help
The pressures well mounted draw attention of such
Too calmly disgruntled one could carefully reflect
Carelessly agonizing and make an entirely problematic hedge

Who am I?

Who am I? Just a little dust that God formed
A being He created within the form of one
Who am I? Just a wee bit sign of life
To spend my life on earth He wants

Who am I? Just a woman or man
Conforming to His commands He plans
Who am I? Just a flower that buds
His beauty is seen and His time is well spent

Who am I and who are you?
We together make up God's two
We are his children and He is proud
We make up his magic and miracles come through

Barriers

Obstacles come, obstacles go,
Once we are moving life will still flow
On a given second, minute or day
Fate comes knocking, without an answer he wants to play
His game is not funny, nor our reaction to it

He continues to dare us to come out of the crib
Some walls can not be broken they never fall away
Others are temporary for a season we're in that state
One thing we have to realize today

Is not to falter just get out of the way
For barriers are shared equally
Fate made sure, we know the tale
The damage fate brings us will hurt, may not stay

We shouldn't forget, where there's a will, there's a way
To still be achieving very successfully
Accept your own barriers, this may be
Easy to say, for dwelling on the negative
Brings more barriers than fate had made

A goal

The mountain is to climb
The hill is there for the practice
The ocean is there to cross
The stream is where we learn of it
So then how can we miss it?

The motive is for the dreaming
The goal is for achieving
Success just starts from trying
While winning not just asking
So then we work towards it

Here lies a mind of planning
For sparing idle lodgings
Engaging and accepting
Recharging after failing
We only reach by striving

But knowing of the challenge
Creating self and dying
Sacrificing not pretending
Can make for one a man
If only he keeps wanting

The enemy within

Within the world in which we live
The enemies are so subtle and sometimes vague
The struggle continues, the sparkle can fade
Familiarity with evil, we watch our enemies' gaze

When being cautious for the out cry of hate
The enemy within wiggles the calculating tricks
Before we know it the enemy within
Has taken our crown and we are stripped with shame

Persistently doomed when the enemy within
Storms out forcefully from our very being
Self destruction is spelled out, we are then very confused
The clock is stopped, the phone is down and the weather surprisingly calm

The enemy within has won from his desires, his very cleverly planned out deeds
We then with our outward claims try to blame any or all but that within
So then where exactly does the problem lie, and what is it we may ask?
No one knows or can tell but the owner of the enemy specifically inbound

Breaking the pattern

There are patterns, and then there are patterns
We adapt one or several and it lingers on
Not knowing it hurts others, it becomes bothersome
It is now a pattern, but we don't realize
Is it then a weakness, a strength or a burden?

Sometimes we see this as a gem
We may use it, abuse it, even be enthused by it
Dismantling then becomes uncoofed a habit
A pattern, we've adapted, weeping in no way
A chore then, a struggle granted this pattern is to break

Stagnation

The past is gone my child, let it be
Fumbling with it is like playing with a wasted cup of tea
The damage done was then not now
So my child please, just let it be
The past lost forever go ahead and let it be

Holding on is unrealistic because it was meant to be
My child, the scar is there it'll fade in time
Pray to God and trust you'll be fine
My child, looking back keeps you behind
While others prosper you waste and whine

Let anger, resentment take no place in your heart
You're not that evil, you're just one of a kind
Look forward little one be wise and clear
There is still hope for the future, you'll see when you get there
My child no one said it was easy in life

If it was said they lied, but in every doing child,
Be calm and patient, it will carry you far
For regretting in practice takes you nowhere
Know looking backward is like being as dead as the residents of the cemetery over there

Going nowhere

The day of judgment rings a bell
No place to hide, no place to check
A circle in the interlope
The judge tells you, how do you do?

Fate winks and sends a smile your way
You wink back but fate turns away
Going somewhere, far away?
The circle has the rounded face

What goes around will come around
Going nowhere and going by the thruway?
The day of reckoning, a day too late
Yet going nowhere, wanting nothing

Flying halfway, learning the trade
Going, going running fast
Going the same way, going no way
And mostly going nowhere swiftly and unattached

Giving up

It is so easy to do
When we have not a clue
No solution to the problem
At least not even a so obvious truce
The best way out we think is
To give up and give in

It is so easy to do
May not be the best answer
But for a brief moment so we think
We may convince ourselves it is the solution
Even if it gives no real conclusion

It is so easy to do
To escape wearing shoes
We walk a mile without compassion
We then give up, we think we know
But soon we still can't find an answer

It is so much easier to do
We feel we have arrived but harm us
We run to something yet to nothing
We see we need to fight with sweat
So then we get up and walk around

For very soon we see
Very soon we know
Very soon we realize
That it is so much better to fight
So much better not to let ourselves down

Addiction

Extremity sometimes can explain complexity
Moderation sensibly determines
No addict's creativity
Temptation so tempting to man's vulnerability

Addiction becomes the proximity
The magnet is go quick
In attracting our attention
Addiction becomes more our action

The effect in due time is a regretting reaction
Becoming addicted starts from a trial in testing
Being hooked an addict looses self and integrity
Easier to do wrong, penalties outweighed

Yes, addict control doesn't save you
Avoiding addiction will remind you

Blaming the victim

We are all victims, don't we know?
Victims of all of life's adversities
If we blame one victim, we blame ourselves
For we are all victims, in the days of our lives
You don't want to be blamed when a victim

Be judgmental if you may, highly critical, rude and say
Laugh to scorn the victim's harm, your day will come
Point for all to see the victim, sneer, mistreat the wounded soul
A ha, A ha, you fool, the very trap was set for you
Remember keenly as you shun and blame and not convene
Your day will come my friend, you will be blamed just the same......or worse

All for nothing...........

We work so hard in our time on the earth
Hoping for the best while moving along with the rest
This is surely an everyday occurrence
Coping, struggling, juggling, surviving

What are the benefits received in our lives?
What do we carry in the end when we're out of sight?
The backstabbing, the lies, the cruelty
The reward is all for nothing on our plate

All for nothing no matter what it is
Only we go beyond the grave
There is nothing that can hold us here
All for nothing we stand wondering in the daze

We may gather a lot in our short life span
With a chip on the shoulder we walk hand in hand
We may hold on with caution those close to our hearts
All is for nought when we step out of the light

If only

If only we could test the tide
Even if we do not ride
To validate and understand
Not quit or try to cry
Observing all the tides that bind
Absorbing the reasons why

If only we could hold the thought
Not back off if its hard
But try to keep the focus well
On all there is that arises
For in this way we feel and touch
Allowing all the best not pests

If only we forget the past
Looking upon today
Reflecting on each and every worthy pace
A course we fully grip
For socializing work and play
A balance it will make

If only we forgive ourselves
For every wrong we've done
Then we could forgive others too
Not hate and make a song
In doing this we've won a case
For maturity will stick

If only we can accept ourselves
Complaining not so much
But openmindedly withstanding all the tests
Trotting on life's road at our best
With our head in not the brewer's bread
We gather up our mess

If only we remember words to conquer in our quest
If only we could gladly see the weight of much unrest
Not hide behind the walls of fear
We'll be our best most often less a valid liscence's mesh

Tension

A strange feeling we get when it exists
We sense it in each and every place
And oh! what a feeling when it disappears
We quickly acknowledge a friendlier atmosphere

What really causes this awareness when tension appears
Maybe intuition speaking to us in spells?
It captivates our emotions sometimes making us fear
For the outcome of tension can bring out the tears

It affects our pattern of thinking the worse of a thing
And yet we welcome not realizing the nervousness it brings
This too is a part of living we still slowly admit
It comes without warnings but may leave us in pain

Awareness makes obvious what this feeling twists
Rejoice when it evaporates and say first a grace
Tension is tension and comes as a part of our plight
So accept that strange feeling and move on with your life

Not only birds have wings

"I believe I could fly" was a song not too long ago
I just don't only believe, but know for sure
Because it is not only birds that have wings and can soar
I too, can soar with my wings I am sure

There is a saying this I now quote "The sky is the limit"
But the heaven is beyond and I nestle on
For it is definitely not only birds that have wings and can fly
As a baby grows so can I, though I am not a baby anymore

I crawl, then walk, fly, and fly way up high
The only one difference, the obvious of us both
Birds wings are visible and mine are not
This doesn't mean that I can't fly and must fail to try

I pop up when I am pushed down,
I will not take underestimation to my head
The more I try the higher I'll fly
I'll soar and continue on every globe
For not only birds have wings and know how to fly

I am human

I am crying, with no sound from my mouth
I am still human, hear my cry
I have eyes and can see
No voice but can speak
I am human, hear my cry

I can not hear the sound from yonder
I can not hear, but I can understand
I am human, accept me
I can feel, touch, love, nurture, like you do
Aren't I as human as you?

I just have a disability, a deficiency
I am not less then you, nor more than you
I am just as human as you are
With my limitations, embrace my talents, my capabilities
Like you, I have some, and like you, I am only human

Unconditional Love

Loving in sickness or in the best of health
Adoring the times of joyous delight
The happy times, the sad times never coerce strife
That is purely unconditional love

When a person is removable in status quo
If an illness keeps one's motor low
Why the tears are shed and the traffic goes
This is also unconditional love

Love is caring, honest and true
Very sincere, quiet and few
An honor received and a blessing returned
This is unconditional love

When followed by works and deeds also
Action never goes out the door
Patience becomes a virtue for two to behold
Love is spelled out and everyone knows

This love is scarce but is there as we know
Seen more than heard for hearing is just a big show
A love not purchased not traded for gold
This love is just there and gladly bestowed

Bloom where you are planted

If you live in no man's land
There is soil to get ready to plant
Still have a dream of a better soil
Even if you have the doubt to sprout

If you land on planet Mars
Knowing life is very scarce
Because you've landed on this land
Find a way to bloom therein

Bloom where you are physically
Biologically bloom when that profession permits
God didn't just drop you and leave you to rot
Naturally find ingredients where you're not lucked out

Tryin' too hard

Don't sweat it big Moses
We ain't going anywhere
Big Moses ain't nothing wrong with the color of your hair
Big Moses ya rushin' the clock ain't at twelve

Big Moses go slowly, ya might as well
Ya have it big Moses it ain't runnin' away
If no one can see it, it'll still be quite okay
One day your legend will be in demand

Tryin' big Moses to get the first prize
If savin' chitlins in the hood is like makin' grits, ya doin' quite alright
Big Moses the Lord got somethin' real good for ya
Don't be so hasty big Moses cuz' ya gonna get it real soon

Mr. Clown

He wears a smile, no matter what
His heart's content we have no clue
He makes us smile, he makes us laugh
He wears that smile for quite a while

Of course, he has his ups and downs
We know not how he copes for the right
The job he has brings peace within
We wonder what his life entails?

He never shows a frown to us
No indication of sadness dwells
We know not why he shares with us
The cheerful spirit that makes our day

Mr. Clown, you see has his problems too
But he chooses to always wear a smile
For he, we would think makes a choice all his own
To smile while making us smile too

The path he chooses as his career
May make us find humor and the joys of life
For pleasantness you see, and I am sure he knows
Receives the better reactions and often grows, this we won't
find in a frown or foe

The happiness pill

Not FDA approved but SELF-APPROVED

1 milligram of pleasant thoughts
1 milligram of faith
1 milligram of perseverance
2 tablespoons of forgiveness
1cup of love with a dash of humor
1/4 of courage
Sprinkled with a lot of hope

Enjoy your pill of a LIFETIME!

Slaughtered

The authority figure while revealing his power
Is telling himself that you have no status
Living as a true representative of deception
Leading you on like he is your loyal counsel

Becoming so comfortable you tend to rely
But boy, how disappointing when you get the surprise
By those who so unsuspecting are found unquestionable

If the evidence of being presumed guilty is wrong
Interfering would not be a healthy but risky preference
Injustice, is it really quite unacceptable?

Ineffective counseling, lack of knowledge, fraudulent science
Harmless error, simple misunderstanding, misrepresentation
Conspiracy, lies and damages like these
Can slaughter a man, denying him his basic human rights
and liberties

A sight for sore eyes

How loudly one hears, but does not listen?
The viewers just watch and are shocked
How old is the vixen whose spirit,
Serves such a sadness about?

The sight for sore eyes is a vixen
Battled by those in a pack
These sore eyes contentment from others
Shows what is forever the plight

How painful, how terrible the damage?
How painful the sorrow to bare?
The evil incredible observant
The losses are numbered and red

A sight for sore eyes but admired
By all watching the foolishness around
As sick and unpredictable the lady
They all seem to help her wear her crown

A sight for sore eyes says the prophet
No senses for a normal life
A fool shaving a magnitude of weakness
Information so revealing of self

Why cry how so foolish soothes the aging?
Destroy and gradually pick up your mess.
A sight for sore eyes, I am not telling
But yes, or no, it may be pending

A road all mine own

I see pebbles in the path
A hidden rainbow out so far
A fear of indecision for the unknown
Holding each pebble in my crown
For a moment, my life disappears right before my eyes

But then I stand by ... still ... wondering
What would my life have been without pebbles?
If it was near a creek or closer to a highway
A paved road or with much more pebbles?

The road I travel is all my own
There is no doubt this was the tune
It is scary, yet comforting too
Whether I travel from every direction

To venture into mines, plains, valleys
To travel amidst Mountains, a forge, hill or desert land
It never seems too familiar this very road
But in many ways, I know it because it belongs to me and me alone

Wait

If the leaves fall wait
As your heart pumps, wait
When love is lost, wait
When the noon comes, wait

In awe of emotions, wait
In praises too, wait
For all glorious occasions, wait
For the Savior too, wait

In waiting stop, look, listen and learn
In earning, love give much, repent
In growing think, send
In all you can serve God

When waiting the struggle gets tougher
When leaning you try not to give in
But with hope, have faith and wait
The sacrifice of Jesus makes hail

And God said "Not yet my Child"

With every desire we ask of Him
He answers each and every request
The timing is not ours to intervene
We only know He has heard our prayers

He allows occurrences to come our way
He permits the devil to overtake
Our patience is tested, our faith is weak
His only response is you'll get your wish

He keeps the line open to communicate
Never allowing us to falter, or decompensate, except He permits
The anger and frustration He knows we feel
Doesn't bother Him any for He is always on the beat

At the moment we feel we've waited a million years we can hear Him say
Hold on just a while longer for my children, I am never late
Maybe giving up is more reasonable, but be not skeptical while you wait
Let your common sense refresh your memory that I created you, all of you
So trust your hearts and be confident that the good Lord will always guide you

"My children" He says, when the time is right
Your prayers will be answered and you all will understand
It is not that I wished to ignore you all at all, it is because to respond to your calls
I am just not in a hurry
Be patient and quite calmly wait each one your turn

So they'll still do the talking

Whatever you do, wherever you go
Whenever you are clothed, or not yet clothed
Let them talk, they often do

Whether day or night or when all is all right
It makes no sense whether you are black or white
For let me tell you even when you are right
Veterans and amateurs all who have a career for gossiping as far as conflict goes
Will injure, not investigate but talk about you

The rain, the sun, the snow, the sleet
In any kind of weather, yes, it really doesn't matter
Quess what, they will still talk about you
Inquiring minds most times want to know
They did of many throughout all walks of life
You being a part of life
What makes you think you don't apply?

What they hear of you they spread, this is to cover their own skeleton and hide
Please, believe it or not, they will talk about you
But let me share with you a thing or two
As long as you live and even when you die
Your likes, dislikes, pains, sorrows, and even joys
They don't care they assume you're queer
Always remember this and be forever sure

People will, oh yes, they will, 'cuz , sure they will
Always, always, talk about you

I can

Here I am with goals and dreams
Beleiving what I ought not to believe
The strength is seen so is the confidence
Knowing that I can, yet scared to proceed

All see the confidence, all see potential
I see blindness and the fears remain
Oh! for goodness sake, how can this be?
In heaven's name, I pray to thee

I can and I keep telling myself
Applying, relating, observing depends
My thoughts focused and I persevere
But yet I hesitate and question with much doubt in me

I can, I know it, I can, I feel it.....darkness no!
I can do what I can, with my dreams
I have hope and know I can leave fear behind
But it seems like something is holding me back and I don't know what

The Silent Observer

He has no word to say at all
Yet he looks and stares expressionless
Not a stutter nor a murmur
Not a single sound uttered
His thoughts are his and his alone

He mixes with others
He gazes all day
With all his observing, he has nothing to say
He doesn't tell if you don't ask him
And if you do he has no comment to make
Never volunteering any story
Even when you ask him, it is just the same story

No words nor a sound or expression he makes
Revealing his thoughts or the deeds he could make
One never knows, and never can tell why he is just
the silent observer as well

I'm moving on

You may call me names
Point to me for all your blames
You may frame me begrudgingly
When you attempt to anxiously gain

You may insult me as much as you want
Set all the traps you most spitefully taunt
Watch me fall and laugh me to scorn
Know if you don't that I'm moving on

Girlfriend, you may steal my man
My friends and all of my plans
I may cry for it will hurt but I'll still stand
Will adjust to the pain but will dutifully remain
But will willingly, gradually still move on

You think you are clever as a fox, one might say
Feel you know which buttons to push letting others watch in dismay
I know it is your goal and your greatest aim
Having a meaningful focus is not a part of your dream

Manipulating, destroying consists of your main frame
Spreading lies instead of love a part of your ultimate name
These things won't stop me nor will it destroy me
For you'll surprisingly see at the very end when the timing is right
And say to yourself with a sadness on your face "my God"!
she did move on

I ain't takin' it lyin' down no more

"An eye for an eye", "tooth for a tooth"
You mess with me man, I'll show you who's who
Harassment, offenses are similar too
All are excuses when you forget the rules
Try to deceive me but I see right through you
Make up all the gravies and call them my stories
When I hear it baby, it ain't goin' to be easy
'Cuz I ain't gonna take too much lyin' down no more
Not even if I done did it many times before

Fiction comes from life's various worries
Some, be it tragedy; perhaps a love story
Interesting issues, we each carry as baggage
It could be worn loosely or seen as our very own cleavage
Yet we cope with much energy complaining with edges
We rise above and fall but our load still carries
That is why I know I need not bear clashes
For conflicts resolved, men grow tall
It is time to eliminate war and breathe sweet talk

No matter how convincing
How devious or appealing
Your nonsense, immaturity, stupidity
All upright, confusing and so very embarrassing
I'm not takin' nothin' lyin' down anymore
And if I didn't let you know
Even if I lied or stole
Whether your plans to harm me are quick or slow
I ain't takin' nothin' lyin' down no more

Life has no guarantees

Life for you and me, has no guarantees
Today you are rich, tomorrow a pauper's creed
Life has no guarantees my friend, most times we do not learn
Today the wealthiest one of all, tomorrow an insane fan

Life is a game some say, some try to play it well
With all the playing and the fair, there are still no certain terms
Life has no guarantees my friend, the fact we often ignore
With all castastrophies around, we still most often crow

Today a king, tomorrow a shepherd, the next day a penniless beggar
Today with homes around the world, tomorrow no home at all
Life has no guarantees with every accumulation are risks
Today we have, tomorrow we don't, and then we are imprisoned forever

We soon forgot when we have much, that we are not in control
The impossible can be made possible and verse versa we too must know
Life has no guarantees my friend, but still follow your goal
Remembering that the assumed can be temporary and easily go

Abuse

Not realized by the abuser, can be
Later in life the damage becomes a blessing
To whom?
The question is asked why? The abused ask
The abuser wonders or should he or she?

Acceptance of the damage, avoidance
Hurt, expressed creates no solution
Anger results, resentment, confusion
So then, who is to blame?
Reason for admittance from whom to who?

Blame becomes fashion
Aggravation, a style, a charisma
Tears a way of life, hidden, discovered
Sparks fly, attention is taken, given
Assumptions and then it all may start anew

With not an answer only a cycle of repeated avenues

Who Could it be?

Are you crazy?
You differ from the crowd
But walk with your head held high
Your goals seem impossible
Your ingenuity irresistible
Who are you amongst us?
Some avoid you, while others snicker at you
You just go by ignoring, being extraordinarily calm

Yesterday, I felt sorry for you
I pitied you from the bottom of my heart, yet adored you subconsiously
You were different, but you had something
Class, character, and style, all rolled into one
You made all kinds of sacrifices, missing all the fun most times
Your personality spoke oh! so loud and clear, yet most didn't see nor understand
You were poor on the money line, but rich in soul, body and mind

Today, I see a different you, a mate that most would dream of too
A more mature person who has left your mockers far behind
Only this time you differ in that you've soared, you've aggressively survived foes untold
You've soared like birds fly way up in the sky
You've let no obstacle deter nor destroy your goals
No evil thing obsess you, you succeeded!
You did not let easy money buy nor attract you for this I am proud
You simply only worked hard, stayed focus and were never crazy after all

Just determined, simply determined to make something good of your one precious life till death.

Quotes

As we live it seems as if we focus more on the money in life than the meaning of life

The gold mine
You are indeed a pot of gold. When you are suppressed, oppressed and neglected. When you are ostracized, ridiculed and misinterpreted. When you are being overlooked and looked upon as insignificant. It is because you have a lot to offer. It is because you are a pot of gold. When the lid of your pot is open it shines and brightens all who see, for you are a pot of gold. When the devil is determined to destroy you and he sends the closest of you to do so, just remember that you are valuable and your value is needed to touch the world in a way no one has done before. You are a pot of gold. Persevere, strive and soar, set your goals and reach beyond the sky because your gold will shine and touch the world. My friend, you are never too old and it is never too late for your gold to shine. One day remember the lid will open not by human hands perhaps not even by your own hands. Then you will see how valuable you are, how rich your qualities are, how very important you may become, you may not be famous or rich. Your value will still touch those it was meant to touch and your spirit and courage will still shine on those you touch. You will leave your legacy behind. You will realize then as you freely look back in time that you were always a pot of gold, never less than that, maybe even more than the purest gold ever found. So be depressed, I say no, be annoyed I say never, have regrets, I say not so. Trust that your day will come, your moment will be, your very life will begin and yet I say begin again when your gold does shine. It will glow from your heart, your soul and your mind. Your body will send the message, your heart sing the song, your soul show the joy and you will indeed be the you that you truly are and were always meant to be, only if you believe.

If knowledge is dangerous, then ignorance is deadly.

Quotes

Run, run for as long as you can. If the road is curvy, run, if it is dangerous, run. Know that while running, if you begin to get out of breath, that is a sign to stop. Not heeding to the warning, if and when you fall, you may never get up.

♥ ♥ ♥

If you believe the sky is blue, it is. If you strongly believe it is any other color you choose, it can be, only if you believe.

♥ ♥ ♥

Burning bridges is similar to destroying one's foundation. Know that achievements are usually derived from hence.

♥ ♥ ♥

In dealing with others, one should practice what he preaches or else judging then is irrelevant.

♥ ♥ ♥

The kindest of strangers is God's way of reminding us that love still rules, if not in the world it does amongst his people.

♥ ♥ ♥

Believing the inevitable is possessing faith subconsciously.

♥ ♥ ♥

If abiding by law is so mandatory and the importance of our rights so constitutional, then obeying our heavenly father should take precedence over both.

♥ ♥ ♥

Your true destiny is determined not by you, or your parents or guardians for that matter, but by a higher power

♥ ♥ ♥

Relying on no one but our Creator is the best decision to make. He calls the shots from day to day.

♥ ♥ ♥

If you are a person without self-worth or self-identity, you are a person without substance

A supreme being is our creator,
our father and definitely our Savior,
he sends us angels, compassionate
lawyers, fret not for now and tomorrow
he will be our lifesaver forever.
Make the effort and strongly
believe, with faith and
hope we will
soon see.

*Never argue with an ignorant man, if you do
he will think he is smart, instead know that no one
knows everything and that includes you.*

No explanation required

Do not answer when not asked a question
There is no explanation required
Do not volunteer to be shot
Know there is no chance you'll stay alive
Weep when tears come fast
Know that there is no reason to explain

Trust if you can in things and people too
Know there is no explanation required
Peace will and can always come again
Because there is no explanation expected
Rise again let not the relapse become plain
Focus on anything or all positive things to gain

There is no explanation required
For the time life's trials have you drained
Drained of woes and dreadful realities
Trust just God and him alone
In knowing all of this and perhaps the latter phrase first
Remember that there is no explanation required

Except by God who already knows your desires

I wouldn't have it any other way

I may not have Emmy awards or Nobel prizes
I may not have fame nor horses and carriages
I may not have tons and tons of finances
Nor gold and fancy type jewelry
I am me and rather not have it any other way

I may not have a worldly title
I may not have brand name clothes
I may never ever dine in high society restaurants
Nor have the contact that may push me ahead
But in my rags I proudly possess a name
As for me, I rather not have it any other way

I have acquired no impressive degrees
For worldly acclaim, but I have a name
No plaques that appear on walls,
Nor name inscribed on buildings at all
I am someone, God's child that's all
For this I am glad and I stand tall
More than anything at all, I rather not have it any other way

An observation

Observe with a vision if you may dear friend,
Know the source of your religion see them much clearer than you
Observe with your ears too my friend,
Know the truth this too brings, it all depends

Observe sometimes based on what you hear
The ultimate truth is sitting somewhere untouched
Observe with your mouth at the victim's expense
Your day is breaking with a spell or special scent

Observe with your hands the touch of a masseuse
The feelings comes naturally and response is like a tool
Observe with your feet trotting onward bound
Leaving failures and successes and everything else behind

Observe with your head as you do all else
Know the source of your religion see the symptoms first
Observe with your heart if you do have one
Caution! observing isn't and may not be always right

But there is always the one who does know the entire attire we wear
Trust and a sense of comfort shown in anyway prove
While the true facts in question are rarely disapproved
All that is true or all that is false no matter how much observing we do

Watching the world go by

I sit by this window staring at clouds
The crowd looks inviting, their jobs are not hard
There is rustling and bustling and noises of herds
Its morning, or noon-day they're singing, they're heard

The pupils are singing, the birds chirps are ringing
The chorus rejoicing with that we're bringing
The lilies are blooming, detectives are laughing
The world is attending the message is sinking

I stand back watching the world go by
I stand here secluded out of the place I had
Reminiscing, dissolving, concluding, regretting
Hoping but knowing that it is all in my past

Watching the world go by
I stand by thinking about all that I could have had
Wondering if the chance would come once more
If I would not do what my enemies have foretold

Heartache of humanity

Little my little we have an aching heart
Little by little it lasts for quite a while
Little by little the feelings subside
Little by little we capture the hour
Soon our aching heart comes back to the norm
Soon we are back and we're not an unknown

The heartache of humans does not choose or trick
It goes first to one man and then to the next
Sooner or later your turn comes and then
Little by later or suddenly life turns
Soon what a blow is felt and a heartache doesn't melt
Soon it hurts, it deeply hurts and you want to bend

Humans we are and humans can ache
Humans we remain and not immune with a twist
Humans we are and feelings we share
Money with bribing can't remove the pain
Sooner or later the pain rips the core
Little by little God heals the sore

Trusting

One confides in those who he feels is worthy of his trust
One exposes his fears and insecurities revealing immense vulnerability
One depends with confidence that his stories will never be told
One's confidant is only human and not a perfect soul

Relying on Jesus is our only hope
He knows it all for richer or poorer
Continue to trust in his unchanging love
Have all assurance for your stories remain untold

The love of God

The Almighty shows us his love
We seemed not to realize it is not as any other
He sends it through others, sometimes not by birds of a feather
Yet it is there, it is always very near

His love is different, it is unique and real
It is abiding, unconditional and not with fear
It asks for nothing in return just extending us a hand
It is endless and given regardless

Searching for this kind of love is not required
There is not a need to seek for something right there
Despite ourselves, this love is there
From the Supreme Being, this is not at all mean

Our best friend, our consoler, our king, our God
This is the only source of this particular love
This is the only love most times we need not crave
It is guaranteed and will be our shield
The love of God to his creation of beings

God is there

When the world has left you far behind
God is there
When your contentment has declined
He is there
When your hope is past tense
He is there
When suffering seems the only exit left
He is there

When trust in mother or father is not high
True to self has gone and ills are not past
When zeal, ambition, cheerfulness is lost
And all the dreams of one is still applauded
Know He is there

When intuition fogs in passing thought
Lost the future of what you thought it was
What was meant to be is now learnt but not so clear
Bewildered you just stand so weak but willfully marvel on
Know He is there

Let faith draw near your armor to behold
Know He is there
Let know man take your crown
He is still there
Pray to your father, He still is yours
Be assured He will not forsake you
So He said

Reaching God

What is his phone number a little kid may ask?
I may want to call him before I die
What will your honest answer be if such a question to you was passed?
Will the answers consist of things you think you already know,
Or do you need an answer to be to him close?

One thing to keep in mind is that, the number is always automatically dialed,
You need not remember it and your call still goes fast
The line is never busy, there is never a queue
You can reach God whenever you pleasingly choose
In your prayers, in your life every day, every night

He is there, He is here, He is always everywhere
So never slumber nor sleep when you cry out to Him
Just holler, or a signal He so willingly seeks
Advices and blessings then are custom-made to your like

They are made specifically to suit His plan for your life
So have hope and continuously reach out to Him
He loves the attention and soon you will see
You'll both remain happy when communication flows deep

Give thanks to God

Thank God each day for the breath he gave
It makes life less complex in each and every way
Give thanks to God for the souls He saved
Whether dead or alive they had souls a gaze

Thank God when you can just for the day
A good, bad, calm or a pretty sad day
Being grateful of no day, means a transition far away
Give thanks to God for the simplest array

Then thank Him too for all of life's complexities
Appreciate, show gratitude, be happy, give praise
For He is the sheperd in every life that lives
Thank God everyday all but three times a day

Those three times are to remind you
So you don't forget to pray
In your prayers keep being focused
On all you do each day

Thanking Him again and forever with everlasting praises

Lord, please soften my heart

Soften my heart Lord, others seem to want it hard
Soften my heart Lord, it is about time I hear thy voice
As my heart softens Lord help me to live allright
Lord renew my spirit as I pray and twice be blessed

Soften my heart Lord if trials walk my path
Soften my heart Lord if witches wand enlightens
As I pray Lord renew my thought and cleanse it
Helping myself Lord, I humbly stand before thee

Clean my heart Lord and make me a blessing to serve Thee
A blessing to others Lord, as I live to please Thee
Save my soul Lord, my weary heart desires
Lord help me with the tools daily please, Lord I beg of Thee

A vow to God

When in your heart you make a vow
Make sure you are sincere
In making this to man or God
Know that you are to care

A vow to man and God differs
But we sometimes don't see
We feel our need for his presence
His vow we often peal

In effort of regaining leaves
But not too far to tread
Obeying God at his command
Is the first of his vow to cling

Present yourself as a living sacrifice
If to God the vow you keep
No shamming for his spirit leads
So in it do in time retreat

Defeated by Sin

Defeat arrives when the sinner is masked
Blindly intruding, the goodness fires back
Self oppression exists, cruelty is quick
Destruction is obvious but the fool is not slick

Oh! defeat not bent nor torn or stolen
The victim is awesomely dwelling beneath
Cries of thanksgiving, sins multiply
Blessings are pouring, sin seems worth while

Amendments are stubbornly absentmindedly wanting
Scares don't come running, fears not descending
Defeated by sin, the lost soul not wanting
Constantly losing, yet not understanding

The still small voice

Within each heart of ours exists
What man would call a gist of grace
It is for each and everyone a still small voice that we usually miss
Some call it intuition, but it is there and causes no confusion

There is a louder voice we hear
Sometimes it clouds the inner voice
Within each heart of ours exists
A heeding to reach out and drift

The louder voice then carries the weight
For no matter what the alternative
It is left with us which one to choose but, oh!
My friend, let's choose carefully, the better voice will make us great

Alone with God

*Loneliness and being alone sound similar but are so different
Meaning being lonely is solved when people come around
The party begins, and on the other hand it never really starts
Feelings may reflect in our mind's vacuum and absorb
Alone we feel and think we're in pain, for there is no one else around*

*Alone with a power that reigns the earth, a strength from way above
Unaware of the peace, the calmness, the stillness, the ease
The unheard contentment, the wide spread acknowledgment and invisible presence
Desperation can never soothe the soul, alone with God we have a goal
A cry from deep within our soul, a hope so near yet quite aware, a sense of loneliness*

*There is none other who can help, but to rest and cry on His breast
After all how sweet the taste, the satisfaction, the joy, the glow
How refreshing, pleasant, unassuming, not ridiculously alarming it heals the sore
Combination of love unknown on earth, alone with God we can live again*

The Bible in you

More is in us to show how God can help others
We are the Bible if we serve the Lord
For those who know Him and those who don't
Our footprints can help more, let's not make it less

Some never get to read a word
They see us as the mirror well
The things we say, and what we do
Determines how they see the truth

Transforming is not our way to live
Examples we can humbly portray
True Godly living is not to only read and pray
But most importantly to be a bridegroom in how we live

The source of strength

God is the source of it all
Depending on Him, our goal
Trust Him and Him alone
He'll never leave us, nor forsake
Bear the cross He did for us

The source of strength
Far more than strength, but the ultimate source
For deliverance, peace, and all we need
The source, for our livelihood, our very functioning

The Lord, our rock, believe He cares
He loves, protects, guides, understands
Believe He cares, listens, forgives, sees
Follow no other, the source is but the only one
The source, our Redeemer, our heavenly Father,
The source of not just strength, but life itself

A source of comfort

Being comfortable when uncomfortable
Expecting most the unexpected
Suspicion elevates each moment and your guard is not yet pressed
Sources usually seem pleasant, strangers wickedness not send

Dreams, accomplishments expressive
To all you defined as friend
Trust lies in no man completely
Only God is the comfort zone

Trusting his unfailing kindness
We can fight no battle all alone
Look up to Him children, just look up in awe
A source of comfort and a peaceful retreat

Moving forward

Looking ahead is miles away
The eyes see it nearer from day to day
Our Saviour He knows it
We want the clue of it
He says "Lay there my child be still don't even think of it"

Marching onward oh! a trying test
Painful memories constantly left behind
Blessed assurance from stranger and soul mates
Snares and confusion from the dearest of enemies
Moving forward is still the way to deal with it

So persistently move forward still
Move forward, onward, however you classify it
Keep focus, keep climbing, don't look back and don't fret it
Each day a new beginning, each night a last good bye, a sort of ending
Move forward on God's plan for you He made it, you must just "apply it"

Tranquillity

How beautiful the grace of God
As He stands in our shadow on Earth and above
An amour of protection a pilot of love
A wall of thanksgiving we nimble the cause

Tranquillity in knowing our Savior
Our true Father above
Brings nations together as He bore the cross
The power more precious than diamonds or pearls
Has led us to look to heaven and not crawl up the wall

A peaceful reassurance

There is such a low lullaby in the garden out yonder
A serene peace not present in a grassy field
If only it could last an entire lifetime
The world will be a much safer place
This precious and solemn calmness waits
Dwelling in the hearts of the child of God
A very deep and holy grace
Apparent love untampered with

A peaceful reassurance is what it is
Remains in tune with no complexities
For how on earth it reassures?
On each and everyone who wears the date
A way to live and learn and wait
A teaching of an example with keen upbringing
Receiving this great peace and calm
Requires only the voice from the divine

In respect of ....

In respect of God we serve Him
In the respect of his grace we love
In respect of ourselves we conquer
But respect of money leads to the grave

In respect of a job we should work
In respect of ambition we conquer
In respect of believing we admit
But the respect of ourselves seems not awake

In respect of pursuing we sacrifice
The respect of which is proven today
In the respect of our parents we obey
Let's respect but respecting ourselves must always lead the way

Fake righteousness

Fakeness plays no part with God
He is real as real can be
Be righteous and rightfully so
Being fake is not what it takes

Reading His word, doing his will
To please Him first not man at will
Look up for He remains
The God for all the universe

Say today and mean tomorrow
The words practiced let it not be in sorrow
Fake righteouness only shows falsehood
Viciousness as a kid, wicked in aging

Don't forget to remind yourself
He is with you not yet sleeping
He is alert in his doing
You too, do your share in his feeding

Love is never a wrong or right,
a true or false, case of sight in broad
daylight, Never a missing fixture or an
unattached tool, the wise and the prudent
all don't want to be fooled, No matter
what people have as their unforgiving
faults, love we must say conquers
them all, love is refreshing for all
involved, it is worth deserving for
the scrambling not a sauce, despite
much failure and ever weird option
it is such a great comfort not bulging
or dying, it keeps the world not
upside-down but just keeps it going
round and round. True love for
many is never lost, no foul played
then to be solved.

A Prayer

A prayer comes in place when Satan tries to engulf you
A prayer is the trick when the odds are against you
When trapped and imprisoned by all the evil forces
A prayer comes handy in places, a reassurance that you are loved

Pray when peace is stolen from you
If peace you had not then let God's spirit guide you
Pray for your enemies more than your friends
For they need the happiness that God always sends

Pray for the joy you possess deep within when betrayed by close knits
Know a clear heart only brings blessings and good things your way
When all is burden don't drain nor strain your life away

Quickly get on your knees and pray to the king

A marriage

We wed today as two strangers becoming whole
For better, worse, sickness or health
To share with each other disasters great and small
For joys that keep on rising and holding us so close
For a future bright and lively that we both will know

Together we are not a twosome, but an entire whole
For separation should never release our hearts which is not old
The love we share between us has brought this marriage vow
We hope to keep the oath of life and love not just a score
The courtship was just the beginning of this great love of ours

As we two stand together and wed this day with love
We hope the love between us be a twosome fold of our faults
When each step taken in our union can grasp the feelings sent
We know we have what others want and hope ours will have no end
For reasons not only to the public seen, we have in each other a friend

His vow

Meeting strangers is a difficult task
Finding you not merely a complex match
I stupidly saw an end in sight, instead of no end
As I madly fell in love with you
Peacefully and calmly you didn't try to leave me
But still I had doubts and a queer feeling lingered on within me
So today I know the feeling of true love
All because I have finally found you, my love
I need not dream anymore
Nor wish for a wife to behold
For you have taken my heart and so today we start
Anew a life together not set apart from each other

My commitment

Sometimes we bomb into our future mates not knowing
Sometimes we never can admit not knowing
Sometimes our focus loses its course
Not knowing we blindly follow
Sometimes we miss our only goal not knowing
In my situation when meeting you I just knew
I didn't have to hold on to not knowing
Now after knowing you I have seen and believe
You are the man that I was meant to know
Not knowing isn't in my heart anymore for with you
I will spend a life of love and behold
With you I truly know that my life can begin as a whole, being complete

Our contract

What God has put together let no man put asunder
Today a life of love and grace
With those we love as witnesses
We make a vow to God and man
To spend our lives together from hence
I can only be grateful for the love we have
I can only want nothing to subside
For God has brought us together
And he will keep us thence
If we can continue to trust in him
Our bond will last and forever bring
Happiness and peace in all our dealings

No regrets

If someone could predict a future without you
I would have to be at a loss of words
But God predicted our prospective union
And today we can be considered blessed
Though from different backgrounds in family and friends
Though in some ways we are still strangers we'll learn
For the bond that brought us to this point
Gives the assurance that we love each other so much
With family and friends gathered here
We can safely express our love in the most appropriate way
We make an oath today and a vow
To cling to each other in all aspects of our lives

Unity

Your beautiful look when I saw your stare
The focus of instant perfection there
The beauty I see when I stare at you
Assures me that you are a beauty too
Now we wed today as friends, but we also do as lovers
So being grateful we have found each other
This is a blessing worth to treasure
A bond that has conquered creating a perfect unity

My good error

Some changes in one's life are for good other's not
Some changes in one's life are bad other's not
Some are permanent and temporary other's are just stagnant
When it comes to all that life has to offer
I could prefer no one but you
Your dazzling smile when we first met assured me of security
And today I stand with you as affirmation that our love is too

Straight from the heart

I love you, I'm concerned about you
I adore you, I'm not lying to you
I need you, I recognize you
I respect and fantasize about you
I won't neglect you but encourage you
When you suffer, I will feel the pain with you

I won't desert you but will hold you
I will pray for you and won't forget you
I am and will be always here for you
Because my heart is leading me to you
All the words I say to you and even how I think of you
Not mistakenly when I think of you it all comes straight from the heart

My heart is beating for you
The sound repeats loudly, louder, louder,
I await your company
I want to hug you, share my life with you
Time means nothing without you
I sincerely miss you

Songs are not music in your absence
So love me back, but I am not asking you to
Nor do I want it as a demand
Listen to your heart, as I listened to mine
So I tell you these words that I am saying to you
They are honestly coming straight from the heart

Quotes

We look up to... and then how does it end in gain and not in pain?

The domino effect, the stubbornness, the willingness, the peace, the joy. All that life provides us on the continual ride of life's journey Here we go

Each day brings about its own, it is clear of dirty or clean footprints. We mark them, as always we do, it may be seen, maybe not, scary! trials and errors

The prize is paid eventually, the effect is realized, the affect we wear, if even hidden. It all begins again, when tomorrow comes, a new beginning, a whole new page

To travel on by the route we choose, unconsciously, subconsciously, sometimes, perhaps not always

We don't know, but we have the opportunity to live today, to the best of our ability, remembering we have only one chance, making the effort to attempt, valuing the moment

Quotes

The treasure of life itself, as trying as it may be at times, it must be lived

There is no certainty in life, but only unpredictability, if tomorrow will come after all

So from the heart to the thought to the action great or small, destructive, constructive, we experience it all

To "think as your heart beats" is the beginning of the gradual ending of your call

Thank you readers!

Notes

Notes